" Oh No, Gertrude!"

The True Story of a Not-So-Naughty Black Bear

by Gabriel Mapel, age 10

photographs by Rodney Cammauf

oh-no-gertrude.com

Interior Design by Gabriel Mapel

Published by:
Wild Earth
PO Box 18
New Hope, VA 24469

800-871-5647
email: info@oh-no-gertrude.com

oh-no-gertrude.com

DEDICATION

For Gertrude, and Denise, and all the bears that have gotten
into trouble because of naughty people.

ACKNOWLEDGEMENTS

I would like to thank all the bears, including Gertrude, another mama bear
of three cubs that I love, a special yearling bear, and all the bears I've
seen, for letting me see them.

I would like to thank my friend Rodney Cammauf for being the photographer
for our book, for supporting my passion with bears, and for spending time
with me watching bears!

I would like to thank my friend Chris Day for honoring the connection I
have with bears, and for the support that she has given me for this book.

I would like to thank my friend Larry Brown for supporting me in my passion
for bears, for spending time with me watching bears, and for supporting me
in writing this book.

I would like to thank all the other wildlife: the deer, the snakes, the hawks,
the foxes, the kestrels, the swans, and all the other animals, for showing
themselves to me and letting me see them while I am looking for bears.

I would like to thank my wonderful Mama and Papa for supporting me with
my passion for bears and for supporting me with writing this book.

INTRODUCTION

Hello!

My name is Gabriel Mapel, I am 10 years old and I am home-schooled in the Shenandoah Valley of Virginia. I visit Shenandoah National Park very often. I love bears and all the wildlife very much. But sometimes it makes me sad when I see naughty people treat them inappropriately. And that is why I am writing this book! When I encountered Gertrude and her three cubs, she seemed VERY mellow. She crossed the road only four yards in front of us! We didn't know it was a problem when bears were used to people. Then a ranger came up and said "Got enough pictures?, I am about to slingshot her to get her to move, she's a trouble bear." We said "Trouble? She seems very mellow!". He said, "Ya, that's the problem!", and explained that she had become used to people and people food, and how that was not okay.

I've seen hundreds of Black Bears in the wild in my life. I have also had a lot of Grizzly Bear encounters, including one at 20 yards on the trail in Glacier National Park, Montana. I have also been very close to a Black Bear mating pair.

I hope this book teaches you how to keep bears safe and I hope that you will be a good person around bears!

In the cold winter months there is no food, so the bears sleep for a long, long time.

Bears give birth to their cubs in their winter dens. One winter there was bear named Gertrude and she gave birth to three little, tiny baby bear cubs! And those cubs weighed less than a pound each at birth!!!

At two months old they had grown a lot, and they looked like this:

When it became spring,
Gertrude and her three cubs emerged from the den,
and the cubs got to see the world for the first time.

And food was still scarce,
so the cubs still highly depended on mother's milk.

At this time the cubs were frisky fur balls
of energy and weighed four to eight pounds each.
And the cubs were pros at tree climbing!

Gertrude depended on meat from deer and other dead animals that she came across.

9

And the cubs would only have a couple of bites.

As spring progressed, they would eat plants, grasses, bulbs, and other things.

And if they were lucky, they would run into an anthill filled with tasty larvae just for them!

As it started to be summer, a few berries began to ripen. Gertrude, and especially the cubs, had to keep eating, so that they would grow to be big and healthy.

One day, while looking for food, Gertrude and her three cubs strolled into the picnic grounds.

And to her surprise, she saw that at one of the picnic tables there was easy to get, free, human food.

Some naughty picnickers had left their food out on the picnic table, and they didn't clean it up before they went out on a hike.

14

She thought that the chips, cookies, bread,
and all the other food was so delicious!

Although some people might think that it was good that
Gertrude got that food, it really was not!

It was not good, because if bears are fed or find unattended food out on the picnic tables like Gertrude did, then they will likely become so used to people that they will have to be relocated or killed.

A FED BEAR IS A DEAD BEAR!

17

Once Gertrude finished eating the food at the picnic table, she saw that at the next picnic table over there was food, too, but there were also people at that picnic table. The people backed up because they were concerned about the approaching mama bear. So Gertrude got all that food, too!

The sad thing is that Gertrude kept repeating this behavior so the Park Service named her a "Trouble Bear." But Gertrude wasn't the naughty one, it was the people who went hiking without cleaning up their food that were naughty.

Gertrude became a habituated bear, which means that she was so used to people that it was a major problem! Then the Park Service had to start slingshotting and paintballing Gertrude, to sting her and to deter her from being in the picnic grounds.

As the ranger said, "I am supposed to slingshot bears and deer who are hanging out in the wrong places, in the hope that the sting from the slingshot will make the animals not want to be in the picnic areas and campgrounds."

Gertrude should just be eating natural foods and her cubs just playing and climbing trees while Gertrude looks for food. But no, they now have easy food, and not just easy food but easy food from people!

One naughty person has put a family of bears at risk! The Park Service is so concerned about Gertrude being habituated because people food is not healthy for bears at all, and if the people at the second picnic table didn't back up and give Gertrude what she wanted when she approached them, then Gertrude might attack the people and she would be blamed and likely killed.

And sadly Gertrude and her cubs do not
stand alone in their situation.

And what the Park Service is most concerned about is what if Gertrude sees somebody on a trail and wants their food? Even if they don't have any food Gertrude might attack them thinking that they do have food. And the sad thing is that when the cubs grow up they will have learned from Gertrude that people have food, so they might get into trouble, too.

Gertrude often strolled into the campground, too, to check out what food might be there. And often bears get into even more trouble in campgrounds than in picnic areas! Obviously the slingshotting and paintballing didn't work. Gertrude didn't learn her lesson. So the Park Service decided that Gertrude had done her things too many times and that they had to move her.

Before Gertrude was moved, she decided to break into a garbage shed in the Park. So she and her cubs feasted on the most tasty garbage!

The garbage was so yummy. She ate bags full of rotten banana peels, leftover pork barbecues, leftover hamburgers, chili, and much more.

The cubs loved the garbage as much as Gertrude did. They thought it was so tasty! Gertrude and her cubs were making a mess, so the Park Service needed to get Gertrude and her cubs to move out.
So they shot a beanbag at her. The beanbag scared but didn't injure Gertrude, but it scared her so much that she ran away from the yummy tasting garbage.

Then it became moving day, so the Park Service cooked a meal in the picnic area to attract Gertrude to a live trap that they had set. And Gertrude strolled into the picnic area and examined the trap, and she even read the sign!

The Park Service put yummy smelling jelly donuts in the trap to get Gertrude to go in, and the donuts smelled so good to Gertrude that she couldn't resist, even after reading the sign. So in she went!

Once they had Gertrude trapped, they still had to get the cubs. But it was not easy to get the cubs because they wouldn't go into a live trap. So the Park Service shot tranquilizer darts at the cubs, which gave them medicine to get them to go to sleep, so the Park Service could put them in a cage and move them.

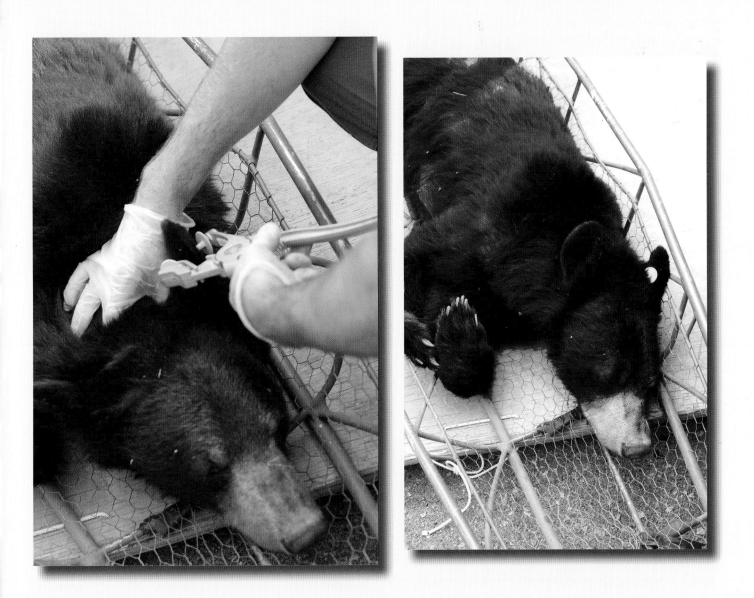

Before they moved Gertrude, they gave her some medicine to go to sleep so they could do an exam on her. They wanted to determine her age, how much she weighed, and to give her a yellow ear tag so they could identify her in her new home. Gertrude weighed 129 pounds and was three years old.

Once they had finished Gertrude's exam, they put her back in the trap on the truck, and they transported her and her cubs to her new home, about 70 miles from where they trapped her.

Once they got to Gertrude's new home, the rangers released Gertrude and her cubs, and the cubs took one last look before running away. Now Gertrude would have to go back to eating natural foods. But if she got into trouble again somewhere else in her new home, then the Park Service would have to trap her again and move her to the National Forest, which would be dangerous for her because it is a hunting area.

The main things Gertrude and her cubs ate after being released were acorns and hickory nuts because they ripen as it gets to be late summer and fall. Gertrude and her cubs had to climb the tall Oak and Hickory trees to get to the yummy nuts.

Although it is usually easy to get to the nuts, sometimes the bears will gnaw the tree branches with their teeth while high in the trees to get to a large number of out-of-reach nuts. And their reward for their hard work is that they get to feast on all the nuts! The nuts are so yummy for the bears, and hopefully Gertrude will think of them as more yummy than people food!

Gertrude and her three cubs were spotted one last time, when they were getting ready to den, and she stood up to take one last look before going off into the woods to sleep for the winter.
And we can only hope that Gertrude will stay safe and never run into any more naughty people, and never run into trouble again!

Tips on how to be among Black Bears

1. Never run from a bear! If you run from a bear, the bear may run after you. And both you and the bear might be in danger, as the bear would be blamed for any aggression.

2. Never feed a bear! Feeding bears puts people and bears at risk. If you feed a bear, the bear will likely end up like Gertrude did, or even be killed.

3. In bear country, never leave unattended food out on a picnic table. If the bear finds food on a picnic table, he will likely become habituated, and this would put him at risk.

4. Never take food into your tent! Bears can smell it. If they break into your tent and get your food, both you and the bear would be at risk.

5. If you live in bear country, make sure you have a bear-safe garbage can. If you leave your garbage out in a regular garbage can, the bears can get into it! Then they could be labeled as "Trouble Bears" for getting into your garbage. And they might have to be killed or moved to a hunting area.

6. Listen to the bear's communication! If they are making huffing sounds, it means they are just letting you know they are there but are not necessarily agitated by your presence. If they clack their teeth (also called "popping their jaws") it means they are agitated. Then you should back away slowly. If they growl or make a growl-like sound it means that they are even more agitated and you have to LEAVE NOW, slowly and immediately. Also, 99.9% of the time if a Black Bear runs at you, it will be a bluff-charge. It would likely be a male bear defending his territory or a sow protecting her cubs. They will almost certainly stop before they get to you. If being bluff-charged, just stand your ground and look strong, but not like an enemy.

7. Never run into the woods after a bear, even for that "perfect picture" or "perfect look." That could scare the bear and it could be dangerous for you and for the bear. If the bear is scared, it could act to protect itself, and the bear would be blamed and possibly killed if you get hurt. Never approach a bear when closer than 50 yards.

Bear Resources

North American Bear Center
www.bear.org
A great place to learn about bear behavior, the colors of their coats, and a year in the life of a bear.

My friend Larry W. Brown's Bear Blog:
www.larrywbrown.blogspot.com
A great place to view awesome bear photos, videos, and learn bear information.

The Get Bear Smart Society:
www.bearsmart.com
The Get Bear Smart Society is an organization created to keep bears safe. They spread the truth, and not the myths, about bears.

"Bears IMAX" movie:
A National Wildlife Federation DVD with great information about bears and amazing video footage of the three North American bear species. In this film, Chris Day, a bear biologist and my friend, speaks from her heart about her connection with bears, and this movie shows her relating with them.

Appalachian Bear Resuce
www.appalachianbearrescue.org
This organization does very important work to protect bears in the southern Appalachian Mountains. They also have lots of great bear activities for kids on their website!

Bear With Us
www.bearwithus.org
This organization does very important work to protect bears in Ontario, Canada. They also have lots of great information on their website about human-bear coexistence and injured & orphaned bears.

Praise for Gabriel's New Book:
My Life With Black Bears

"Gabriel Mapel is a talented young naturalist with an astonishing connection to wildlife. Through years of careful observation, he has gained an unparalleled first-hand knowledge of the lives of Black Bears as individuals. In this remarkable and awe-inspiring book, Gabriel gives us a unique chance to look inside the world of these magnificent animals."

— *Kenn Kaufman, Naturalist and Author of* Kaufman Field Guides

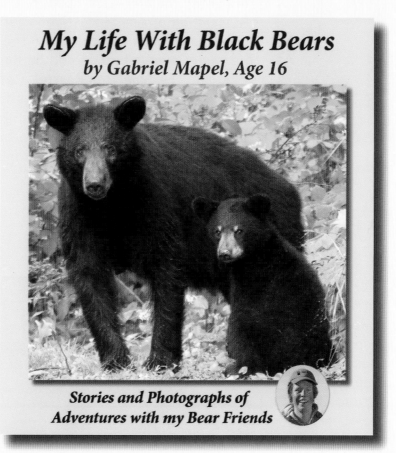

My Life With Black Bears
by Gabriel Mapel, Age 16

Stories and Photographs of
Adventures with my Bear Friends

Since writing **"*Oh No, Gertrude!*"**, Gabriel has continued to observe, study, and write about his experiences with wild Black Bears. At age 16, he wrote his sescond book, **"My Life with Black Bears"**, in which he shares his stunning photographs of Black Bears and accounts of some of his most amazing experiences among them. The book is an opportunity to learn even more about the lives of wild Black Bears, and it inspires and encourages us to do our part to make sure these amazing animals are better understood and protected. This book is available at Gabriel's website: **wildwithgabriel.com**

About The Author

Gabriel Mapel is a 10-year old home-schooled boy from the Shenandoah Valley of Virginia. He loves bears so much and he wants to help keep them safe! Among his other interests are: birding, photography, hiking, camping, playing guitar, astronomy, and much more. Gabriel is an accomplished astronomer, having earned his Silver Messier Certificate from the American Association of Amateur Astronomers at age 8. Gabriel also appeared in an episode of the TV show "Zona Latina." He really enjoys birding and he has many favorite birds, including the American Kestrel, Red-tailed Hawk, and Mute Swan. Gabriel's aspirations for his future include becoming a Shenandoah National Park bear technician, taking over his father's business, going to Mars, becoming a professional photographer, and seeing more bears all around the world!

About The Photographer

Rodney Cammauf has over 35 years experience in photography all over the world, starting as a teenager with a Kodak Brownie camera and developing film in a neighbor's basement. Rodney's images have been used by magazines, newspapers, television, government, and commercial enterprises. His latest assignments have been for the Everglades National Park, National Park Service, and the Institute of Wildlife Sciences.

Rodney believes that through the appreciation of the beauty of wildlife as well as understanding wildlife and the environment more people will be willing to support the agencies and organizations dedicated to the management and preservation of these valuable resources. See more of Rodney's work at:

www.rcammauf.com